M's Musings

By

Myrna Griffith

Scriptures marked (KJV) are taken from the KING JAMES VERSION (KJV): KING JAMES VERSION, public domain.

Scripture quotations from The Living Bible copyright © 1971 by Tyndale House Foundation. Used by permission of Tyndale House Publishers Inc., Carol Stream, Illinois 60188. All rights reserved.

Cover Designer: Bob Ousnamer

Name: Myrna Griffith
Title: M's Musings
Identifiers: ISBN: 978-1-953114-12-9
Subjects: 1. Religion / Inspirational
2. Religion / Poetry

Published by EA Books Publishing, a division of
Living Parables of Central Florida, Inc. a 501c3
EABooksPublishing.com

Many thanks to my helpers

Leanne Campbell

Mary Montanaro

TABLE OF CONTENTS
M'S MUSINGS

View From The Sideline

My Story-----My Faith

(A study in contrasts)

My STORY has alternately been an open book, divulging too much personal information or a blank page, afraid to reveal, fearing pain.

My MIND has been a clear blue sky, only to turn into a dark, dismal gloom.

My EMOTIONS have felt like a fragile floating feather, changing to a heavy hammer blow.

My LIFE drifted on a gentle breeze, caught by surprise by a ferocious hurricane.

My SPIRIT has soared high on the wings of hope, then I've lost my grip and plunged into the depths of despair.

My SOUL has been touched by Grace and then scorched with fire.

Through all those polar contrasts, as far back as I can remember thinking consciously about it, my faith has always been focused on the Lord, even when it was difficult to see beyond my own nose. (Even before I knew it was the best thing for me) In retrospect, I can see the distinct pattern of God turning my life around, inch by inch as I gave up the reins of control.

My STORY book is becoming more and more open as I share my faith with others.

My fears no longer have the power to overcome my courage.

I know my once worrisome EMOTIONS are accepted and affirmed by God's Grace and I am free to float, knowing that I will never fall so far that we can't handle it together.

My MIND can now accept the clear bright days and the dark dismal days as equal partners in God's wonderful world.

I now have the strength to disallow any ferocious hurricanes on the weather map of my LIFE. I choose the gracious gift of the gentle breeze to soothe me.

The wings of hope have kept me going when I couldn't find anything else to hang on to; carrying my SPIRIT ever upward.

My SOUL, now that has endured a whole lot of all-encompassing "bad stuff" not worth wasting time or energy on, but the Grace of the Lord has sustained me, helped me survive and I have learned great and valuable lessons along the way.

My Prayer

Dear Lord, I pray that you will use this Holy education, my many blessings and the gifts you've bestowed on me to mold me into a fine-tuned instrument in your orchestra of life.

HUMOR

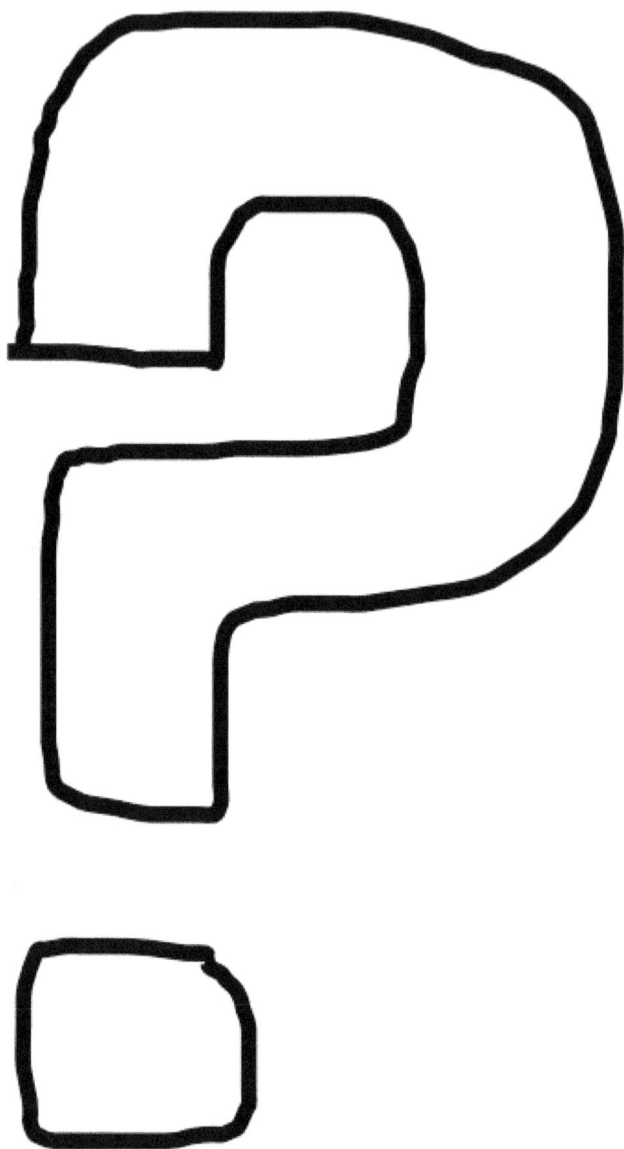

WHAT?

What shall I write about now?
What shall I write about?
What shall I write?
What shall?
What?

LIFE

Life is not for TAKING
rather for GIVING
and also FORGIVING those
who TAKE from others.
For in FORGIVING
we also RECEIVE
and therefore HAVE
no need to TAKE

A ROSE

Someone said
"A rose is a rose is a rose is a rose"
But not to MY nose to my nose to my nose
When the fragrance of roses is
Borne on the breeze,
A rose is a sneeze is a sneeze is a sneeze!

With

Without, without, with is out.
Out without with is also out
With all due respect
We thus can detect
With is the winner throughout.

BROKEN TOE

Oh No, Oh No. I broke my toe,
But to a doctor did not go.
It was a pinkie one, you see,
So Myrna fixed it, 1, 2, 3.
Four Band-Aids taped it up real tight
and kept it straight both day and night.
T'was on a Thursday, this last one,
and I had things that must be done.
It hurt like blazes, that old toe,
But there were places fun to go.
Key West beckoned, a show to see.
Friends drove and walked slow for me.
A great show, "Hot & Soul, by name.
"Julia Nixon" of "Dreamgirls" fame.
I can drive and I still can work,
But walking makes my toe berserk.
So far it won't allow work shoes
To press against its well bruised blues.
Wish me luck, for time is flying.
Got to go, no time for crying.

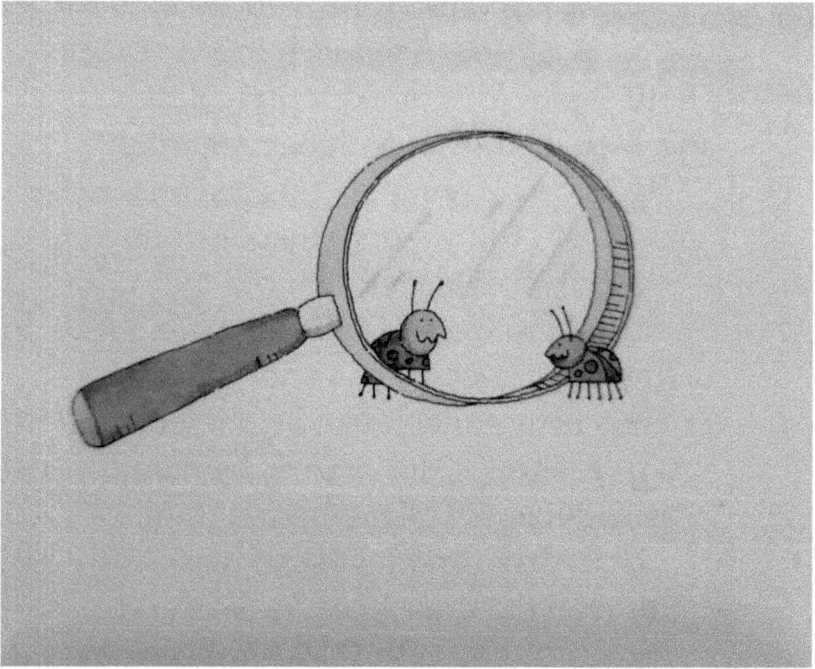

I'm a Bug

(exercise in one sentence)

My story began under a rock in a garden one warm summer day when a nasty slimy worm came wiggling too close to me and dislodged the rock just enough to let the air in and sunlight which in turn shocked me out of my lovely sleep and made me roll over to shade my eyes which motion caused me to wake up completely so I sighed and resigned myself to the new reality or fate whichever it might be and struggled to my knees and rubbed my eyes as I crawled out from under my safe haven only to find that it was not as warm as I thought it would be so I scampered off in search of something to wrap around me to ward off the cool breeze until I could adjust to the surprising change in temperature only there didn't seem to be much available in the area so I hurried over to the greenhouse in search of help which might be found there and to my surprise I found a pretty yellow garden glove which must have belonged to the lady of the house who spent many hours in my garden so I crawled into the safety and warmth of the glove and gratefully went back to sleep.

From The Crones' Nest

Don't pity us when we're old and alone.
Look into our eyes, they're not sad.
Our path has reached the realm of the Crone.
Look deeper, you'll see that's not bad.
Our way was full of both pain and pleasure.
Many are the lessons we've learned.
Passing through grief to peace beyond measure,
Our place in the nest, we have earned.
From up here the view makes life seem clear.
There's so little time to waste now.
Each moment a blessed gift, so dear,
We make the most of it somehow.
Do you wish for a comforting word?
Does your heart ache with heavy woe?
Let us listen so you will be heard,
Without fear that others will know.
Is your life filled with tribulations?
Confusion not easy to take?
Can't find any clear situations?
Our thoughts might show which choice to make.
Do you want to laugh or need to cry?
Afraid someone close might see?
In our aerie there's no one to pry.
You can do both and feel free.
Is there a need for quiet in your life,
But you can't find it on your own?
Come, let us help, for dealing with strife,
Is something not feared by a Crone.

BUT

Crones aren't all heaviness, so beware.
There's lots of humor tucked away.
We've had our share of "devil-may-care".
Laughing is fun, so we say.
It's not that we are smarter than you.
Intelligence plays a small part.
But our "been there-done that" list proves true,
We're ahead by miles when you start!

FAITH

And now, although Ten thousand enemies
surround me on every side,
I am not afraid.

Psalm 3:6

(The Living Bible)

FAITH

No sense to life?
No signs of hope?
Life is so unfair.
Only failure.
No success.

Where is God?

<u>My faith is fading.</u>

Is He right here listening to my fears and despair,
Showing me sense which I could not see,
Brining me hope that I saw no signs of,
Telling me He'll protect me in this sometimes
Unfair world?
<u>My faith is getting stronger now.</u>

Above all……He is helping me to expand my
Mind, heart, and soul.
To find success in feelings not felt before,
Areas not seen before
And personal worth not realized.
<u>My faith is whole again!!</u>

I'm in God's hands with nothing to fear.
Thank you, Lord.

You ARE **<u>my sense.</u>**
You ARE **<u>my hope.</u>**
You ARE **<u>my life and</u>**
<u>My Success.</u>

1990

When I think of the wisdom and scope of His plan
I fall down on my knees and pray to the Father
of all the great family of God –
Some of them already in Heaven
and some down here on earth –
That out of His glorious, unlimited resources
He will give you the mighty inner strengthening
of His Holy Spirit.

Ephesians 3:14-16
(The Living Bible)

Daily Prayer

Lord,

Help me to utilize my belief in your promises to…

Fill my deepest hungers, desires and aspirations.

Take away my worries about the future, others, and myself.

Make my convictions more enthusiastic.

Make my life and my witness more spirited

And make my dreams and visions more exciting.

Shape and mold me according to your plan

And help me find the path which You've designed for me.

Let me experience peace and harmony as I travel through

This earthly life

An instrument in Your grand orchestra,

Yet still a child in Your humble family.

Amen

Don't worry about anything;

instead, pray about everything;

tell God's your needs and

don't forget to thank Him

for His answers.

If you do this you will experience

God's peace, which is far more wonderful

than the human mind can understand.

Philippians 4:6-7

(The Living Bible)

AGING RAVINGS

Do I have a choice?
Can they hear my voice?
How can I rejoice?

Nothing else rhymes.

Is there sense at all?
Will I rise or fall?
Let's dance in the hall.

To best of times.

What shall be my fate?
Sit around and wait?
Open up the gate?

To hear the chimes.

What is left for me?
Bobbing in the sea?
Can they hear my plea?

Who can I trust?

Shall age not be kind?
Havoc comes to mind.
Medicine I find,

Prevents my rust.

To thyself be true?
Doctors' orders do?
Rebel and then subdue.

Adjust, I must.

God has the answers.
God hears you.
Trust God.

Oh, yeah ..... I forgot

25

CHILD IN NEED

I am in my little boat,

Sailing out to sea.

It's taking me so far away

That no one can hurt me.

God will take me in His arms,

No human will be near.

God is steering my little boat

Through storms I will not fear.

Psalm 23

Paraphrased by Myrna Griffith

Because the Lord is my shepherd,

I have everything I need.

He lets me rest in the meadow grass and

Leads me beside the quiet streams.

He restores my failing health.

He helps me do what honors him the most.

Even when walking through the dark valley of death

I will not be afraid,

For He is close beside me,

Guarding, guiding all the way.

He provides delicious food for me

In the presence of my enemies.

He has welcomed me as His guest,

Blessings overflow.

His goodness and unfailing kindness

Shall be with me all my life,

And afterwards I will live with Him

Forever in His home.

ROAD TO GROWTH PRAYER

Lord, please grant me the strength
and grace to push on down the road
called "growth".
Especially when the rewards are fogged
in illusion,
when I feel so ill-prepared,
when I recall how often I have failed in the past,
when my intellect misleads me,
when my emotions confuse me
and especially when other travelers interfere.

I will praise the Lord no matter what happens.

I will constantly speak of His glories and grace.

I will boast of all his kindness to me.

Let all who are discouraged take heart.

Let us praise the Lord together

And exalt His name.

Psalm 34

(The Living Bible)

DANCE OF JOY

"There is no happy life, only happy days."
I didn't write those words, but I certainly can relate.

When I look back upon a period of time to see if it
was happy,
My opinion depends on the mood I am in at the
present time.

If I am happy, the mood acts as a doorway to all the
good times.
Those invited moments join hands in a delightful
dance.

If I'm sad, the same action takes place.
Negative memories queue up at another door
And arrogantly sashay in.

How fortunate that these two paths are so far apart,
With only one entrance for each and no connecting
doors.

As long as I understand this to be a normal
occurance,
I have faith there will be many more dances of joy
to cherish.

For just as the heavens
Are higher than the earth,
So are my ways higher than yours,
And my thoughts than yours.

Isaiah 55:9

(The Living Bible)

BITTERSWEET

(for a dear friend on an anniversary of his wife's death)

This day is marked with sadness true,

As you morn the loss of love.

No heart can feel it as you do.

Except our God from above.

And so a rose I give to you,

A token to show I care.

The love you had I know was true,

A gift not all get to share.

You've been blessed by Him, we both know,

And I feel He's blessed me, too.

Near this date fifteen months ago

Our friendship began brand new.

God's plan is still a mystery

And we only play the roles.

Doors opened, closed the history

We all share with other souls.

I am leaving you with a gift ---
Peace of mind and heart!
And the peace I give isn't fragile
Like the peace the world gives.

John 14:27

(The Living Bible)

Sleep Denied

My mind is troubled at this time
By things I cannot see.
Perhaps if written down in rhyme
Its sense will come to me.
Though it's not clear why sleep won't come
I have no cause to fret.
The lessons from my past are some
I've only half learned yet.
Like ghostly raiders passing through
My hard-won peace to steal
The happiness I felt was due,
To question if it's real.
Familiar words enter my head.
The truth helps me endure.
'This, too shall pass', I've heard it said
and I have proof, for sure.
The menace weakens as I write;
Its strength no more a threat.
For it is wrong and I am right.
My soul has paid its debt.
I'm closer now, recalling when
To Him in grace I turned
So I pass through sleep's gate again,
My sanctuary earned.

She is a woman of strength and dignity,

And has no fear of old age.

When she speaks, her words are wise,

And kindness is the rule for everything she says.

She watches carefully all that goes on

Throughout her household,

And is never lazy.

Ecclesiastes 31:25-27

(The Living Bible)

View from the Sideline

The player is benched.
No play today.
Have to sit and watch the other teammates do the job.
How frustrating this must be to a young team player.
I caught a glimpse of that feeling today.

After church, I sat with my cup of coffee, munching on a cookie.
The panorama in front of me was full of wonderful busyness.
Happy busyness that I was once a part of.
Busy-ness that is now being done by a group of others.
The new church team was preparing to go out and feed the many needy people in our area.

The simple example of reasoning for this is that I am older now.
Deeper into that explanation, though is sometimes other things.
After all, some of those 'do-ers' are older than I am.
So, age is not always a given factor in the ability game.
No, age isn't always the reason we sit, viewing life from the sidelines.

For many of us and in my case there are other reasons
we can't keep up anymore.
Without going into detail and offer the dreaded TMI
"Too much information"
I'll just touch on them.
They are all elderly medical and involve chronic pain.

Many folks who have known us for a long time
don't always understand
why we aren't our old active selves.
Do they assume that because we are only in our 70's"
we should be able to do more?
Do those who don't know us think we are just lazy;
watching everyone else work;
not bothering to help?

But they don't know, do they?
God has blessed me with some friends who DO KNOW.
He and I know who they are.
I hope you have some, too.

So, I will sip my coffee and munch on my cookie
here on the sideline.
God and I know I have done my part in the past.
I can relax and enjoy being the spectator now.

INSIGHT

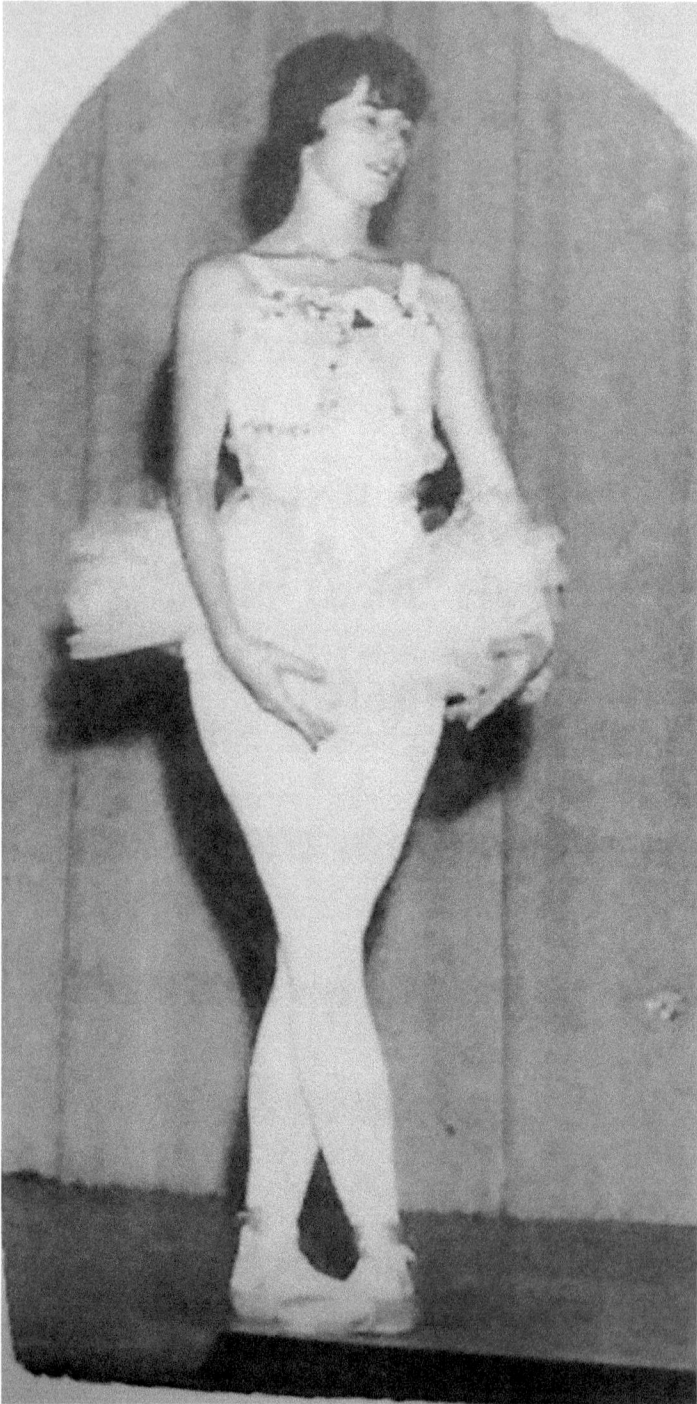

This story was written in 1955 for my Junior High School newspaper

*my very first to be published, so it's quite unpolished.

(As I look that far back in my life, this is a solid reminder of what it was like to be a teenage girl, eager to please, willing to perform, hoping everyone would like her.)

WINGS ON HER FEET

"One, two, three and four. One, two, three. Hold it!" yelled the tall, dark instructor, his eyes glaring.

"What's wrong with you? Loosen up. You look like a walking pogo stick. Try again."

"One, two, three, four. That's better."

'He is as bad as the clock on the wall; never stopping but working and working.', thought the tall, slender, fair-haired girl working to the beat of the instructor's baton.

As the old clock struck five, her thoughts were suddenly changed. Time to change into street clothes and become an ordinary person again.

Working with Ivan was far from working with a human. He was always crabbing or slamming his fist down on the poor old card table. How he treated Ellie, like a robot!

Weeks and weeks went by with the same ordeal every day. Up early in the morning, and I mean early. Then working, working and more working until five o'clock at night.

Finally the big night! As Ellie walked up the steps in front of the fully lighted theater, her knees began to shake and her heart started pounding.

She thought of all the work she had put into this and suddenly her thoughts turned to Ivan, so mean, so cruel, never smiling.

'No time for that now. There's much more to do!', said Ellie to herself.

It was the stagehand's yelling, "Ellie, you're on" that pulled her out of her dreaming.

Could she do it? Well, we'll see!

The lights dimmed, the music started and out she twirled. All that was on her mind was to dance, and dance, she did!

As she turned and twirled, she glanced into the wings. 'Could that be Ivan?', she thought. 'No baton in his hand, and what was that?' A smile, it couldn't be.

But it was. He was standing there beaming with pleasure as she had never seen him before!

Now she danced as she had never danced before. I think you know why.

THEN AND NOW

There were times in my life when I felt like I was on a roller coaster.

Sometimes a different one every day, each new and scary, but exciting. The thrill of the ride would carry me along, wrapping me in the protective blanket of youth.

As time flew by, I came to realize that the thrills of new and different could leave me with an emptiness and a longing for peace and tranquility.

I gradually settled in quite comfortably to my current carnival ride. A roller coaster in slow motion with lots of ups and downs, but not fast enough to ruffle my heart beat.

Some days, I do miss the excitement, though.

This item was accepted and published in the Providence Journal in 1995

*different last name... former marriage

This early riser does it her own way, in her own time

SOME PEOPLE think I'm crazy. After all, what woman in her right mind would drag herself out of bed at 4:45 a.m. when she doesn't have to be at work until ??

Is this necessary? Well, that depends on what you call necessary.

My problem? I hate to rush. My day doesn't seem to go well when it begins with the stress of hurrying. In my book, a bad start equals a bad day.

I can't remember when this allergy to hustle started, but it seems to be getting worse as I grow older.

I discovered the joys of early rising quite by accident. For two years, I got out of bed early to start a 7 a.m.-to-4 p.m. workday for a company 40 miles from my home.

When I found a better-paying job in the local area, naturally I thought I would be able to pick up at least one extra hour of shuteye. At first, that proved to be true, but before long, I found the new career more stressful than I had anticipated.

I started dreaming about it at night, and soon I began waking up earlier and earlier. My first thoughts were work-oriented. How to solve existing problems; how to ward off future ones; what to do and how to act. Dire scenarios rambled, unwelcome, through my mind.

I even got to the point of contemplating the unthinkable ... quitting. That solution wasn't high on my option list. I had to think of some ways to cope.

Then, I remembered my past morning commutes. The traffic hadn't been too bad, and I'd managed to fit a decent breakfast into the schedule, so.

A psychologist would probably call the strategy I came up with a form of stress management. I prefer to call it simply, "My Time."

First, let's qualify that 7 a.m. starting time. What that really means

is getting to work by 6:55. It's a race to beat the clock. I wouldn't want to lose the precious 10 minutes I'd be docked if I punched in at 7:01. I know, rules are rules, right?

Well, as the saying goes, a rose is a rose, too. This woman needs some time to smell one or two of them before I face the drudgery of an eight-hour workday ("Their Time").

So . . . after my eyes are open enough to function, I set about my daily ablutions as quietly as possible. Next, I dress by flashlight, so as not to wake the love of my life. (Note: This works best if you lay out your clothes the night before. This is the point where opposite personalities can feel free to call me a fruitcake. I understand.)

The hardest trick to perform quietly is rummaging around in the kitchen and refrigerator for the lunch I didn't have time to prepare the night before. Oh, well, I'll just have to take care of that somehow during the glorious, relaxing 30 minutes the icons of industry call lunch. (Oh . . . make that 20 minutes. I forgot about the 5 minutes standing in line at the time clock and 5 more for a repeat performance of the morning card-punch procedure.)

Gosh, it's 5:30 a.m. already. You'd be surprised at how much more time it takes to get things accomplished when you're trying to be quiet.

I'm not so sure the neighbors are thrilled when I start my car that early, but no one's complained yet.

their internal engines started.

By the time I leisurely walk out, I weave through a throng of nervous clock-watchers, running late and in a frenzied rush to grab at least one cup of coffee before their work day begins.

I get my choice of parking spaces in the factory lot. By the time I punch in, I'm relaxed and feeling ready to tackle the day with a positive attitude.

When I contrast that with the way I feel on those mornings when my inner alarm clock has failed and I'm rushed, there is no doubt which I prefer. I can't say this would work for everyone, but I know I'm happier when I start relaxed.

"My Time" is not only important — it's necessary for this working girl's well-being.

Myrna Witherell lives in Attleboro, Mass.

Fortunately, my faithful old Chevy is usually as ready to roll as I am. The fact that we early birds are still in the minority also means there is less traffic to deal with.

Where do I go? Well, it took a little scouting around, but I found a few cozy restaurants that open up about that time. I pop into my favorite place, pour my own first cup of coffee, and settle down in the seat of my choice, armed with paper and pencil for writing, crossword puzzles and the sections of last Sunday's newspaper that I didn't have a chance to read. (Just in case I'm in the mood to do anything with them.)

More often than not, by the time my well-done bagel (with the cream cheese I deserve) is served to me around 6, I just sit back, enjoy and watch as the colorful parade of kindred souls trickles in to pick up that magic brew guaranteed to get

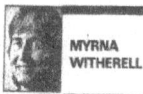

MYRNA WITHERELL

46

SOME PEOPLE think I'm crazy. After all, what woman in her right mind would drag herself out of bed at 4:45 a.m. when she doesn't have to be at work until 7?

Is this necessary? Well, that depends on what you call necessary.

My problem? I hate to rush. My day doesn't seem to go well when it begins with the stress of hurrying. In my book, a bad start equals a bad day.

I can't remember when this allergy to hustle started, but it seems to be getting worse as I grow older.

I discovered the joys of early rising quite by accident. For two years, I got out of bed early to start a 7 a.m.-to-4 p.m. workday for a company 40 miles from my home.

When I found a better-paying job in the local area, naturally I thought I would be able to pick up at least one extra hour of shuteye. At first, that proved to be true, but before long, I found the new career more stressful than I had anticipated.

I started dreaming about it at night, and soon I began waking up earlier and earlier. My first thoughts were work-oriented. How to solve existing problems; how to ward off future ones; what to do and how to act. Dire scenarios rambled, unwelcome, through my mind.

I even got to the point of contemplating the unthinkable...quitting. That solution wasn't high on my option list. I had to think of some ways to cope.

Then, I remembered my past morning commutes. The traffic hadn't been too bad, and I'd managed to fit a decent breakfast into the schedule, too.

A psychologist would probably call the strategy I came up with a form of stress management. I prefer to call it simply, "My Time."

First, let's qualify that 7 a.m. starting time. What that really means is getting to work by 6:55. It's a race to beat the clock. I wouldn't want to lose the precious 10 minutes I'd be docked if I punched in at 7:01. I know, rules are rules, right?

Well, as the saying goes, a rose is a rose, too. This woman needs some time to smell one or two of them before I face the drudgery of an eight-hour workday ("Their Time").

So...after my eyes are open enough to function, I set about my daily ablutions as quietly as possible. Next, I dress by flashlight, so as not to wake the love of my life. (Note: This works best if you lay out your clothes the night before. This is the point where opposite personalities can feel free to call me a fruitcake. I understand.)

The hardest trick to perform quietly is rummaging around in the kitchen and refrigerator for the lunch I didn't have time to prepare the night before. Oh, well, I'll just have to take care of that somehow during the glorious, relaxing 30 minutes the icons of industry call lunch. (Oh...make that 20 minutes. I forgot about the 5 minutes standing in line at the time clock and 5 more for a repeat performance of the morning card-punch procedure.)

Gosh it's 5:30 a.m. already. You'd be surprised at how much more time it takes to get things accomplished when you're trying to be quiet.

I'm not so sure the neighbors are thrilled when I start my car that early, but no one's complained yet.

Fortunately, my faithful old Chevy is usually as ready to roll as I am. The fact that we early birds are still in the minority also means there is less traffic to deal with.

Where do I go? Well, it took a little scouting around, but I found a few cozy restaurants that open up about that time. I pop into my favorite place, pour my own first cup of coffee, and settle down in the seat of my choice, armed with paper and pencil for writing, crossword puzzles and sections of last Sunday's newspaper that I didn't have a chance to read. (Just in case I'm in the mood to do anything with them.)

More often than not, by the time my well-done bagel (with the cream cheese I deserve) is served to me around 6, I just sit back, enjoy and watch as the colorful parade of kindred souls trickles in to pick up that magic brew guaranteed to get their internal engines started.

By the time I leisurely walk out, I weave through a throng of nervous clock-watcher, running late and in a frenzied rush to grab at least one cup of coffee before their work day begins.

I get my choice of parking spaces in the factory lot. By the time I punch in, I'm relaxed and feeling ready to tackle the day with a positive attitude.

When I contrast that with the way I feel on those mornings when my inner alarm clock has failed and I'm rushed, there is no doubt which I prefer. I can't say this would work for everyone, but I know I'm happier when I start relaxed.

"My Time" is not only important — it's necessary for this working girl's well-being.

Myrna Witherell lives in Attleboro, Mass.

TELEPHONE 1

They're very cold machines, I feel

Like taped messages on a reel.

Words and words to communicate,

Name, time, places and date

My heart has so much more to say

That can't be heard in this cold way

How better suits me to a "T"

To have you here instead with me.

TELEPHONE 2

Telephones feel so cold.

Answering machines are like little hollow boxes

Shouting out orders to say words you'll understand

In what ?????   5 minutes?

I sigh and hang up.

Hurried words won't do for this call to you

I just can't seem to emit

The warmth and feeling that I want to give you

Very frustrating for my heart

that has so much to say to you.

Does anyone have a pen and paper?

AUSTERE LIFESTYLE

My lifestyle some misunderstand.
To them it seems austere.
Missing all the important things,
That they all hold so dear.

Their houses big and beautiful,
Landscape top of the line.
I'm content in my neat one room,
The set-up suits me fine.

SUV's, minivans and trucks,
Needed to get things done.
For my needs, in comparison,
A compact car do run.

New clothes for this and clothes for that,
At work, at home, at play.
I buy when mine wear out, that's true,
But seldom big bucks pay.

Movies, concerts, plays and travel,
Are great for all who go.
I've done my share of all those things,
Still do with folks I know.

Material things are valued,
Collections to compare.
I have everything I need,
Around me everywhere.

Cape Cod Railroad Bridge

I could see it over and over again,
Yet eagerly gaze anew,
To catch the sight of the crossing train,
As it plays its part on cue.

It patiently waits while the bridge horn sounds,
The giant weights ascend,
The great spans high pitch screech abounds,
'Til the downward journeys end.

The length of tracks grinds to a stop,
A whistle blows; train's ready,
The tension mounts, as clank, clank, clop,
The engines course is steady.

The final car has cleared the span,
The tracks ascend once more,
The weights return to where they began,
All looks the same as before.

The bridge alarm signals, "It's all clear. "
And water traffic will reign,
'Til the time arrives which I hold dear,
When this scene is mine again.

The wait between is a pleasant one,
My spirit enjoys renewal,
The Cape Cod Canal in cloud or sun,
Is a multi-faceted jewel.

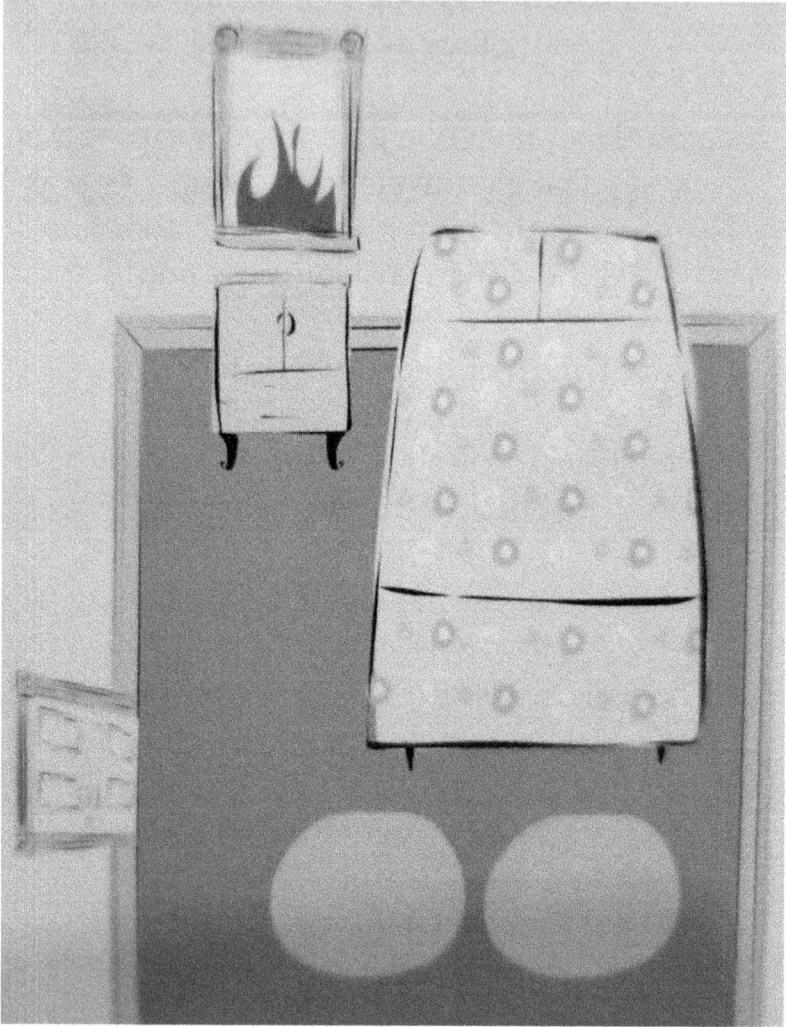

COCOON

My soul sometimes feels threatened by the modern
world
Which seems set up to belittle or totally ignore true
Spirituality

But alas, I must deal with it every day.
How?
I retreat to my cocoon.

I am a fragile butterfly,
My imaginary cocoon becomes a sacred place

Where I can safely
Think my thoughts,
Say my prayers,
Enjoy my memories,
Record my visions
And write my dreams.

Gramma's Daffodils

"Da-fo-dih, da-fo-dih"
Pretty yellow faces waving up
from the bottom.
I am at the top.
I don't know why,
but I'm up here being carried around,
held tightly, but in a gentle way
that feels oh, so good.
My carrier keeps pointing
to things and making sounds.
I like da-fo-dih
the best.
I think my carrier does, too.

OLD, OLD, OLD

Why were children taught to fear
the old one down the way?
"Strange old crone", folks spout when near,
Young ones hear what they say.

Growing old, they learn to see
makes you mocked by many.
"Won't let this fate come to me;
no I'll not have any."

Hard and fast youth works and plays,
Old age a distant threat.
Thinking that one of these days
That curse they'll conquer yet.

There was a time way back when
The words like 'crone' meant good.
Even hags respected then,
Not hidden in the wood.

Wisdom valued, treasured, too
Experience worth gold.
Honored by all, healer true,
No disgrace to grow old.

But time flies by unnoticed.
Life catches by surprise.
The best laid plans all blow kissed,
Away fades the disguise.

All at once, old age is here.
No way to push it back.
Reality crowds out cheer.
Life's train is right on track.

Time takes on its self-made pace
Reflection now worth more.
Honored knowledge finds its place.
Spirit comes to the fore.

Crones and hags with wisdom blessed
Have watched the scene unfold.
And now the young put to the test
We all get Old, Old, Old.

REMEMBER, MOCHA?

The familiar tail knock on the floor,

The many walks along the shore.

He cheered you up when you were sad.

He kept so calm when you were mad.

Always there and patient, too,

He changed a part of your life for you.

Do you remember, long ago?

He's the nicest friend you'll ever know.

INHERITANCE

What should we leave them'
Our loved ones and theirs?
Cash is the first thought,
To settle affairs.

If only we could peek,
Into their thoughts to find,
The most memorable thing,
Which brings us to each mind.

Oh, wait now, let us give,
That a tad more thought.
Our search could open up,
A case we'd rather not.

What a disappointment,
It would be to learn,
Of memories that prove to be,
Not for stuff we yearn.

Better then, to carry on,
The best way we know how,
And give them all the love we have,
Not later on, but
NOW!!

*And just one more ...

KUDOS TO OUR CHILDREN

Our children did not choose to be born.

They could not choose their family or the childhood they had.

They had to make their own way

through the hazardous path of connections and society.

Now they deal with myriad issues and trials of their own.

They owe us nothing.

Hurrah for our children!!!!!

MYRNA

I was born on May 15th, 1940 in St. Luke's Hospital in New Bedford, Massachusetts. My parents were Ernest Edric Griffith and Eleanor Jenney Howard Griffith. I am their only child. My first home was a lovely farm in Fairhaven, Massachusetts owned by my grandfather, Henry Thomas Howard and grandmother, Grace C. Cowen Howard.

Back then it was still a busy working farm, complete with cows, pigs, chickens and many vegetable lots. I say lots because they were much bigger than the gardens we see today. A sawmill sat across the road from the house where my great grandfather had cut and sold lumber. My mother, also an only child grew up there in the days when it was such a large farming operation that the barn was full of cows, acres of corn grew, and my grandmother also fed farm hands in addition to my mom and grandfather.

At that time, my dad was traveling to Springfield, Massachusetts every day to work at Monsanto Chemical Corporation. Fortunately, he landed a job in Attleboro, Massachusetts. Mom, dad and baby Myrna moved to a 2nd floor apartment in Attleboro. Shortly after that, my mom contracted tuberculosis and was brought to a sanitorium on the outskirts of Attleboro.

I was very young, so I don't have any recollections of that stretch of time, but by the time I was a toddler, Mom had recovered, and we moved to a large apartment near the hospital, still in Attleboro. It was a neighborhood bustling with children of all ages to play with. We had a large garden, of course and also chickens. My dad's specialty was tomatoes.

My parents had their hands full with this precocious bundle of energy. My first brush with the law occurred when I was four. A few neighbor children and I were playing house and decided to take a walk downtown (probably my idea as I had walked it many times with my mom). I was the mother of course. When we reached the center of the town, the highway department was painting the lines of the crosswalk. My little group stood and watched until the trucks rolled away. To our surprise and delight they left lovely little flags to keep people from walking on the fresh paint. There were so many of them we decided to pretend to buy some, and each picked one up and started back home.

We only made it to the second block when a police car drove by and parked up ahead of us. Not realizing we had done anything wrong, we proudly yelled "Hi" and waved our new flags. He was a nice jolly man, laughing hard as he approached my little group.

I don't recall exactly what he said to me, but I knew immediately I was in deep trouble. The word "steal" was the one that shook me up the most. He escorted us all to our homes and as I was the real culprit, he came into our house to confer with my mom. I spent a lot of time in my room for a while after that. I still have the article that was printed in the Attleboro newspaper about the incident.

We moved again before I was five. This time it was a two-bedroom apartment on the ground floor of what we called a double-decker. The owners, an elderly doctor and his wife lived upstairs.

I was enrolled in a lovely morning nursery school a few blocks away from our house. Once again, my precocious character tested both my parents and my teacher. I wonder if the other students were secretly entertained by this rebellious bad girl who spent a lot of time sitting alone on the stairs in what is now called a "Time Out".

One very good thing came from that year. When I was behaving, or chose to, my talent for music, dancing and singing blossomed. As luck would have it, the same little school was used in the afternoons as a dancing school. My parents judiciously signed me up and there began my love affair with dance. By the time I was a teenager, I was teaching both ballet and tap.

Pre-teen babysitting brought out the story telling, and the writing bug began with a short story (about a ballet dancer, of course) published in my Junior High school newspaper.

My first attempt at writing a novel came after a friend's dare. Then followed a writing course and the submitting of "Westminster Puzzle" (a murder mystery) which received many rejections. I was fully aware that would be the case, but one favorable critique that came in along with some suggestions convinced me I was on the right track. Westminster Puzzle is still waiting for me to rewrite it, but instead, novel number one, "Stowaway in Time" (a light fantasy) was published.

After a few years, my creative energy renewed, "The Catch" (another murder mystery) came into being and was published.

If you are reading this collection, you know I'm still at it. My programs and church services for my fellow seniors have come to a halt due to the dreaded pandemic. There are a few more stories started, all waiting to become my next novel, but.....................

A ghost story entitled, "Skezulah" seems to be the next one calling me.

Photo Credits

All photos unless otherwise noted are used with permission of author from her personal albums. Myrna Griffith

Cape Cod Railway Bridge used by permission of David Witherell pg. 54

All clipart from Broderbund Print Master   unless listed below:

> https://publicdomainvectors.org/en/free-clipart/Professor-teaching/42322.html

> http://www.clker.com/search/question+mark/3

> https://publicdomainvectors.org/en/free-clipart/Sailboat-and-sailor/43325.html